MAPPA MUNDI

Philip Gross was born in 1952 in Delabole, Cornwall, grew up in Plymouth, and now lives with his wife Zélie in Bristol, teaching Creative Writing at Bath Spa University College. He has worked with every step on the educational ladder from nursery to PhD, is a Quaker and a horror writer, balances his poetry and fiction with work for radio, the occasional stage play and children's opera, and enjoys collaboration with musicians, painters, dancers and writers of all kinds.

Since winning a Gregory Award in 1981 and first prize in the National Poetry Competition in 1982 he has published books with Peterloo, Faber and Bloodaxe, including *The Air Mines of Mistila*, with Sylvia Kantaris (1988: Poetry Book Society Choice) and *The Wasting Game* (1998: shortlisted for the Whitbread Poetry Award). Poems from all these and several small-press collections are brought together in *Changes of Address: Poems 1980-1998* (Bloodaxe Books, 2001). His latest collection, *Mappa Mundi* (Bloodaxe Books, 2003), is a Poetry Book Society Recommendation.

His poetry for children includes *Manifold Manor*, *The All-Nite Café* (winner of the Signal Award 1994) and *Scratch City*, all from Faber, who also published his first novel for young people, *The Song of Gail and Fludd*, in 1991. Since then Scholastic have published five more; his first for Oxford University Press was *Going For Stone* (2002), described by *The Guardian* as 'wonderfully scary and unusual'.

PHILIP GROSS

MAPPA MUNDI

BLOODAXE BOOKS

ISBN: 1 85224 622 7

First published 2003 by
Bloodaxe Books Ltd,
Highgreen,
Tarset,
Northumberland NE48 1RP.

www.bloodaxebooks.com
For further information about Bloodaxe titles
please visit our website or write to
the above address for a catalogue.

Bloodaxe Books Ltd acknowledges
the financial assistance of
Arts Council England, North East.

Cover printing by J. Thomson Colour Printers Ltd, Glasgow.

Printed in Great Britain by
Cromwell Press Ltd, Trowbridge, Wiltshire.

For Zélie:

Love, be flagrant and delicate,
a riot of tact, the careless falling-
into-place exactness of it all.
Be the singular coupling, the lingering
lightning strike, the solemn giggle
loud-hushed, through the midnight wall.

Be the tink of ice cubes on the edge
of melting in an equatorial heat;
the sun, downed in one gulp, pops up
to a raucous crèche of parakeet

and howler monkey: ancient cries,
today's news in the forest canopy,
same difference, the first time again. Us?

I-and-I, as Rastas say. That singularity.

Acknowledgements

Acknowledgements are due to the editors of the following publications in which some of these poems first appeared: *Acumen, The Bridport Prize anthology 2001, The Laurel Review, Leviathan Quarterly, London Magazine, Modern Painters, The North, Outposts, Poetry* (Chicago), *Poetry London, Poetry Review, Poetry Wales, Rattapallax* (NY), *Signatures, Smith's Knoll, Stand, The Reader, The Tabla Book of New Verse, Thumbscrew, The Times Literary Supplement, Verse* and *The Water Log.*

Thanks are also due to the judges of the Blue Nose competition, 1999 (for 'The Plunge') and the Tabla competition, 1999 (for 'Icelings'); and to Zélie, above all.

Contents

In the beginning...

...it's six in the morning
and no one at home. The world
appears, all its things in it,
imprinting your sight with its skyline.
the street with its stray dog, its sheaf
of free newspapers furling off – all there
from the start like Adam's navel

or a set for a film never made.
Call it Atlantis, call it Lemmingtown:
Bank Holiday, they said, and up and drove
west, west to the end of the known road
and off. Or drank themselves to sleep
together on the stroke of midnight
stepping straight from Auld Lang Syne

into one-apiece afterlives
and look, left the morning like a note
unsigned, and you sweeping the street
and you calling up stairwells, you
walking into anybody's room
unasked, finding *everything* there
for the taking, a burglar's bad dream

because where could you stash it?
It would need a warehouse as big
as the city, precisely, as available
as 6 a.m., as vacant as To Whom
It May Concern. You could wall yourself in
with everybody's leavings, sole heir,
in a kind of pyramid, a kind of tomb.

Walking the Knife

(for Medea Mahdavi)

She looked out on her childhood garden; a late frost
had turned the leaves to knives. See the crack in the door
with the moon looking in? That's the knife.
The knife is no news of home on the evening news;
the knife is *waiting*, and a siren getting nearer in the night.

The knife is a straight street, glinting, sharp with rain;
it narrows towards the horizon; it can cut both ways;
the knife is no toy for a child; the knife-
sharpener looked in from the street as if he knew me
and when I said I had no knife he only smiled.

The knife is an old song that no one can translate now:
we walked three days without water on the plains of the knife:
even the word 'knife' might be not be right;
the knife is a letter that hides in the alphabet; dangling,
the phone flex is a species, cunningly disguised, of knife.

A package from the old world, sealed with tacky-tape
might be the knife they've sent for you, but how to open it
without the knife? Look, there's blood on the white
page – just a paper cut, so quick you never felt it;
the most innocent things can be friends of the knife.

The knife is lion-coloured mountains, seen through shivering acacias;
the knife is hunger in the middle of a meal with friends;
the knife is not *either…* nor *or*;
the knife won't take *No* for an answer… or *Yes*;
in the wrong town, on the wrong night, the knife is not a metaphor.

My mother's knife's handle was inlaid with lapis lazuli,
a clasp in the shape of a swan's neck; still it was a knife;
the knife is the last word: 'well?' And again
we're walking the knife edge, on towards the tip; if we
can keep our balance that far, we'll know what to do then.

Amour-en-cage

The first bite is with the eye;
the next, with the name of the thing
   and the price. Such jewels of rare
   fruit, in a Bath-stone booth
on a Regency bridge, one room
you see right through to the drop
   beyond, to spray mist rising
   from the weir, the sound of it
like turbines of an ocean liner.
Step in off the street, my dear,

   to a whiff of quince, the perturbation
   of the door chimes. Touch the crisp
sound of these crumpled Chinese lanterns,
each with a waxy sun inside: Physalis
   or *amour-en-cage*. Take note
   of those who shop alone,
their brooding on each purchase: winter-
sunset-pink persimmons held to the light
   as if looking for the flaw. Or couples
   (one's hand on the other's waist,

a half-resisting moment on the doorstep),
how they pore over sorb-apples, bergamot,
   bullace – him glancing up, struck
   by some delicate matter of fact
like how she lifts a – what, you can't
make out; the season's fading – not
   quite to her lips, not quite to touch
   that tender place under the nose
which small children, comforters clutched
tight, stroke, stroke and fall asleep stroking.

Icelings

Stop, one foot on the ice;
it winces. A grey
bubble bulges, near and pale
as a face at frosted glass,
then it shivers away:

twenty pieces of quicksilver
smuggled downstream
into storm drains, lightless
ducts, a gulping outfall
into creek mud

or the concrete culvert
by the ring road, the condemned
well in the garden
barred in for the children's sake.
So one by one by one

they come: the legionary
from the skirmish in the bog,
slipped free of rotted harness,
rust stains running clear;
the poor murder'd maid

of penny dreadfuls, the *Police
Gazette*; the village-fair Houdini
who was going to buck
the odds and make it
to America with one last trick;

and paler than any, the souls
we chose not to let slip
into life between us.
Not reproachful, hardly sparing us
a glance, they'll be travelling on.

Tree-frog fingertips
under the ice, they pluck
small bright berries of air
to press them to their lips.
Once, just wanting to help

the sluggish blurry carp
to breathe, I cracked a frozen pond
and found them dead of the shock.
No, melt it gently
and abide not knowing

if the face you half see
will come clear
or dissolve with the ice,
leaving black water dragging,
dragging under and too chill to feel.

Plunge

(Mackenzie River, Vancouver Island)

One moment, whitewater slews past a stone beach,
all surfaces, slapped back and forth with the light
    then it narrows to deep,
      subdued as in a green–blue
waiting room. Zigzag sunlight goes tickertape down.

All the skies the glacier must have drunk,
miles up, are concentrated here: tattoist's ink
    pricked into folds of limestone.
      Small pools going scummy with heat
breed tadpoles and a skim of greenish flies.

One harebell dithers in a crack too fine to see,
in no breeze, maybe dowsing what the water
    won't say openly. I've doggy-
      paddled, gasping with the cold
burn of its tongue, towards a bend where suddenly

the surface stretchmarks. Haul out, quick. And peer
over a boulder where it trims then curves out –
    a fifty-foot fall, still too solid
      to splash, one thud
of impact. And there on a ledge, three taut braves

in boxer shorts have left their primrose camper
in the lay-by and gaze down into a plunge pool
    black with depth. Let's have you,
      it says. No good looking
at each other. One, first. Now, which will it be?

Spoils of Acre

What relics have you, stranger,
from the Holy Land, what
Instamatics? One:

an inner window to an inner room,
a courtyard folding in from courtyards
that we never entered. Two: a moon made of sand
going down in the sea. Three: thin waves
torn off slowly
the length of the lighthouse wall.

All that, and somewhere, underfoot, the rumour
of a high ribbed vault, of not-yet-
echoes waiting for the seep that gathers
like a pressure, gathers
to a drip
            to fall.

            *

A bowl of trapped blue,
       running wave-tips of Arabic script,
          a pool upended but unspilled:

the dome of the Al-Jazzar mosque
       holds all the sky you could wish for.
          Outside, the small loud dusty world

is full, too full from any angle...
       Beneath Mameluke walls, a children's
          play-assault-course, loose torn scrolls

of rubbish and a football pitch...
       Beyond which, olive uniforms,
          no skyline unwatched, regular patrols.

            *

Its layers build on layers, like an oyster shell –
whitewash on sand-brick, concrete underpinnings,
mopeds, donkeys, aerials, overhead wires,
and under all, a brackish smell:

the sea leans on the sea walls. Inside, stone
glooms built like Gothic forests. The Crusaders' hold.
There is a whole cathedral, buried. There are some
vaults sealed and best forgotten, known

or guessed at by a hollow feeling, like the sound
of your heart when you wake in the night
with an echoey drop inside you. Acre.
Here and there a staircase leading down.

*

Now they come through the ramparts from the coach park,
    you among them, blinking in the glare and heat
        and the skirmish of *here-my-friend-I-show-you*

guides getting up from small coffees and headlines'
    quick turbulent script, moving smooth
        into languages *hello guten tag shalom maybe*

I show you Crusade vaults sir none of others know of
    take you to my own home special come with me.

*

All hallowed, the dead knights were shipped to Burgundy,
to France, to England – all clean bones.
How do you suppose they did that?

With the scrum of cooks, whores, horse-doctors, barber-
surgeons came the butchers, tanners, tallow-makers
scooping froth from boiling vats,

teasing white bones from grey meaty scum.
Came street dogs, came the seagulls gathering
from downwind with the same sea cries

you'd hoped to hear, Sir Knight, at landfall, sailing home.

*

Forget the Jerusalem
dream. This is the sword tip
snapped off but impacted
in the desert's flank. Scar
tissue. There are older
ruins: Roman columns
just lying there, so
what? There will be more.

*

When the guide we'd failed to shake off for an hour
precisely stopped and demanded hard currency
we were defeated; no, we didn't have the heart
to haggle or protest or meet his eye.

The sky of the mosque wasn't ours to take,
not at any price. On the sea wall a bride and a groom
were arranging her veil in the wind.
The once-for-ever photos. Then back in the car.

And us? We got to keep the thing we never
saw: grit and plaster dust frittering down
in the dark, their small tish endlessly remultiplying
and outside, seeping down, seeping in,

the less-than-insect whittlings of voices...
Whole courtyards have been known to vanish
without warning, like a heart can stop,
the street-crust is so thin.

Damp, Rising

For all our makings good, for a lick
and a promise of plasticky off-cream
gloss, woodchip on top, it smudges back
like a hurt round the eyes, like the dream

you gradually know you're in, again.
The autumn brings it up (the house
won't sell) like mist on long-drained
Levels, trees up to their knees, cows

legless, eerie-unconcerned, the ground
remembering its life as floodland,
and the M5 sunk, its undercurrent slowed.

Like that, or like a face beyond belief,
a poor exposure on the holy handkerchief,
the sweat-marked bedsheet of the Shroud.

The 1 a.m.

The eager desolation
    of the lit vending machine

in the bus station's unmanned
    all night snack stop puts

me in mind of *Hi-I'm-Jonah* who
    tried to give me religion

by peeling his sleeve back: *Friend*
    I want to show you this –

a bleached scar, needle punctures. This
    is what I mean by Saved,

what do you say to that, see,
    there's nothing you can say...

The 1 a.m.
    pulls in out of nowhere. Some few

touched in by the vendomat's glow
    come to resemble a queue;

they wait as the coach debouches,
    then mount; they frame their faces

one by one, in dim monochrome,
    in the high square windows.

As the coach draws out they're gazing
    not so much at as over

and beyond here as if past regretting,
    while these others, new-

received, with homes to get to, can't
    help glancing back and you don't

have to stand here many nights to notice:
    all these faces we're so proud of,

1 a.m.,
        we wear them much the same.

Long-loaders

(Kamloops, British Columbia)

Would anyone live here if they didn't have to,
this sage-grey plain between two ranges

that sunrise or sunset can suddenly touch
long shadows from, loosed like a spillage of oil?

It's some kind of calling, how each bush
is pricked out too-sharp and particular –

a landscape you'd want to write home about
and do, and do, until you realise this

is home, for the duration. That shack
at the end of the scratch road blowing back

into the hillside, grit to grit, a failed mine,
that's a kind of calling. Its mineral bloods

still stain the gullies, as livid as rouge,
a dry old come-on. Elsewhere *is* what

it must have promised. Halfway over,
you can start to lose it, dreaming equally

of pine-dark coast-lipped forest, stony inlets
clucking in the night, redskin arbutus limbs,

or of flatlands stunned by abundance of grain.
And trains come, one a day, from there to there;

you see them, an hour away, rounding the hillside
on a contour, threading through avalanche shacks

where screes run: hundred-truck long-loaders
with engines front, middle and back. You can wave.

They come and come then, like families
grumbling but complete, clank by, clank by

so long you think there'll never be an end of it.

Like Knives

In the attic where we led each other
for the last act of the dream
glints, first,
then the edges of things
stepped out of the shadows, limb

by limb, slick steel, a cold storage
of surgical bric-à-brac: a throat-
doctor's lamp
on its stainless mount, clamps,
kidney dishes, certain instruments

on trays, a probe of moonlight
on the single bedroll, on us
at it like knives
between the nitrous oxide cylinders,
the castor feet of iron sided cots

not built for babies, wheelchair axles,
calipers that dug into our flesh;
we didn't care,
in deep amongst each other's folds
like a scrabble of hounds on the scent

at the fox's earth, like a mobbing of gulls
for slops flung from the trawler's stern
with a clatter of gear,
the glint and slither of the stainless
fish gutted live on the deck

as we landed the catch of each other,
hauled out of our elements...
Whoever's dream
this was would have to wake, we knew.
For now, we lay there gasping.

Gulls Mating

(Newlyn)

The first step's a balancing act
on a bungalow chimney, one up
on the other's back, impassive, staring out to sea.
    It could be the start of a record-
    breaking stunt, hoopla,
    a pile of twenty! Then

he hitches his wings, he hangs
himself up on hooks, and it's me
not them who sees the way the light combs through
    his spread flight feathers,
    filmy. He trampolines her,
    he shimmies his tail

and I think of the school pool and life-
saving practice and keeping two heads
above water, as she cranes hers sideways, back,
    as you did when we arched
    together, me inside you
    snug that way and yes,

it's just a feeding reflex, this fencing
of beaks, from way back in the nest
before they fell out on the air – as they do now,
    and so must we. But
    see, it takes their weight
    and holds them, more or less.

Glass House Days

There are days when the sky
is cold blue glass. OK,
you know there's nothing
really *blue* up there,
it's in our eyes, us blue-eyed boys and girls,

but the sunshine looks
so hard and near
you could throw a stone
on impulse, smash: midday
in splinters all round, and off the world's

edge, vertigo, the not
of up and down. So care-
ful, on brittle particular
snow, we pick our way
with blue shadows. There must be Inuit words

to help us but we have no way of saying.

An Opening

Or you spot a way through
between two shadows five storeys high;
      one is Duckett and Thomas Co. Importers,
      one an investment opportunity
that promises twenty penthouse flats
somehow in a couple of years but now
      there's only a slam-top skip between them
      and a scorched paint and vanilla smell,
and a particular dog that has rights
to be here, he'd have you think,

and what beckons you through
is a dead-end of abrupt surprising light,
      a warehouse weightless as an after-
      image of itself, going straight up
to the empty-handed grain hoist
and straight down to what
      seems hardly water, that cuts through
      this brick world, with no surface
but the milk of slight mist, moving
like the silk skim oil might give.

All this, compelling as a roadblock
that you can't turn back from, not now:
      they'll have seen you, they already know
      more about you than you do yourself
though you can't see their faces, only
the light that clothes them, and of course
      you'd walk towards it, wouldn't you?

Tryst

November: unforgiving rains
and the weir is an overshot mill wheel.
Its V gullet makes a point of foam

sharp as heartburn, forging upstream
underwater making for the shadow
of the bridge, its cutting edge a frill

dragged out to choppy froths
of silt and streetlight, like a bad
thought, troubling the undertow.

     *

He rams it back up the alley.
Kills the engine. Sits, just the chrome
of the grille like the grin of a conger

from its rusty pipe. It's the waiting
gets him. Think of a service station
starting with A... through to Z. Or else

you'll go berserk. Too soon, that is.
Once the business kicks in,
fine, it's just a job, like anyone's.

     *

Five children, fissile from McDonalds,
way past bedtime – Hallowe'en,
there's scarlet sauce on everything,

chips, sundaes – and a bat mask,
skull mask, Quasimodo and the tried
smile that a glum dad wears

thin, as they lag and straggle on the green
man crossing. One small Dracula drags,
slips his grip
         (What he'll hear
in his mind, long after, is the weir, not
the tyrebite and rev.)
            as the man goes to red.

Thin Places

A drawn breath: the cusp
of an hour... Overhead in the tower
something gears, something tenses;
the bell bows its head to the clapper
ready to accept the blow

that does not fall. You look up
and the puddle-glassed librarian
is looking up, too, straight at you.
Where his eyes should be is see-through
like the age-spots in a mirror.

Or think of a blown bubble wobbling
down the staircase of air
in its crinoline, down the spectrum
till a black spot, pure
transparence, grows and grows,

a thin place. Thinness:
there are pockets of it in among the stacks,
the un-books. With a quiver
one blinks out; its story has slipped
into being, a life takes a turn

while the volumes in waiting resettle
and sigh. Hush. In this long-held breath
the least sound could be critical.
Flip a page, it's a whipcrack,
it could raise a panic,

shelves emptying like the frilled
arc of a cardsharp's shuffle
breaking ranks in mid air, a free-for-all
free fall every way but down,
moth-blurs of pages coming at you

straight at you and through
so the small print reads inside you,
you in it. There's your face
like an enemy's, staring from the frame
of some life; there's a bed

behind you and on it, all angles
and mute accusation, some lover
you've just turned away from
to stare at the mirror, as if
it might relent and let you through.

The Drowned Book

A summer so dry
   the bracken crackled
      like twigs in a fire.
The fields grew blond,
   hopelessly flyaway.
      Around the reservoir

heatwaves walked
   the crazy-paving
      mud like revenants
of stink. And then a gable
   showed, a hint first,
      then accumulating evidence:

a wall rendered with silt
   raised slowly like a wreck
      for fear of sundering;
a door in its frame
   that had fallen out whole;
      the roof slumped in,

but gently, off its greasy
   stays. It took a week
      before the blister crust
might take a child's weight.
   The youngest, lightest,
      got there first – the first

for thirty years. Peered
   in. Thin mud drapes
      like dust sheets. All
moveables gone, but
   in the corner, a square
      stone sink, still full

to the brink and – he'd swear,
  years later – as he brushed
    the surface, something pale:
a book. (How long had they had
  to load the cart, the waters rising?
    Sunday-dressed for the sale,

the neighbours, condolent
  as crows...) Pounds, shillings,
    ha'pence, farthings. As he touched
the columns shivered, the fine
  lines of profit and loss
    dissolved and he clutched

nothing solid – a swirl of scurf
  as the water grew milky and,
    for such a hot day, oddly cold
and when the others found him
  crying, there was no proof.
    Nothing he could hold.

Talking Stick

'The lies of the poets are lies in the service of truth.'
JOHN OF SALISBURY (*d.* 1180)

A once-in-a-lifetime
present. Fifty dollars, and keep mum at Customs.

It's a hollow human
marrowbone. The work of small bone-beetles.

See the single hole
where the eggs were drilled in, laid

in the fullness of time
to hatch, feed and, too plump to exit,

die. Their husks
sift when you tilt it, like dry rain, a gust

of ash, the *hist!*
the village liar-for-a-living used to still

a circle in a clearing
in the forest night. And when a child

was seen to sicken
with the hollow-bone, he would be waited on

like a visiting dignitary,
be approached as you would a doorway

with a crack through which
you dare not look, through which the Nearly-

People might seep in
with news, lungs not made for this air

breathing *Listen...* Listen.

Coromandel

Some days, the faint rim of the Inner Ranges;
other days not

or all you see are clouds gathering inland
meditating weeks of rain.

Now they come down the slopes towards you
like old Orthodox priests with their censers

sprinkling the just and unjust with unwanted blessings
and their dour plaints, basso profundo:

muddy-minded malodorous monx.
But without the visitation how would they grow,

your pumpkin vines and four colours of gourd?
Dogs loll their tongues and flop tails to and fro,

too hot to do more than watch lizards like tricks
of the light flicksilvering up the doorpost.

Still new to this shore, that's how you find yourself:
between the quick of lizard and the slow

of pumpkins which are plentiful and cheap and oh
    to be a plump slow pumpkin vendor
    with a plump slow pumpkin vendor's wife
    and a packing case stall, change in your hat
    and a call of O, O, O...
                O is for Only, for Over and Over
                Open Seas where the grey sails go

    Oh he looked from the drawing room window.
    He looked up from troubles and toast.
    He saw himself setting off clockwise
    but he never got far from the coast.

               *

They've all got mobiles now, the loungers in the square
with brand names like wings at their heels.

No wonder: the public wires are sagging
and the switchboard heavy with old news.

Half the lines they connect you to are pre-war.
Which war? Don't ask. Who knows

what old collaborations, old informings
still stain the gutters between families?

Better ask nothing but the price of lemons.
Chance the café with the fusillade of table footie.

Let yourself expand into a big round gaze
like a baby's, puffing out and up till, oh

> *Oh he swore by the drudge of his demon,*
> *he swore by the court jester's ghost*
> *that he'd make it to somewhere by sundown.*
> *You'll still find him there by the coast.*

*

Faint news from England. Some late friend's
grandchildren have sold off the family name

and withered in the cost of living.
The packet boat comes but vaguer every day;

you can see right through it – see horizon
and strange slim bright sailboard sails.

Besides, what wouldn't they charge
such an old cask of words for the portage?

So angle your easel for what's left of the view,
still there, framed by scaffold and cranes.

The cats roll on the concrete, swat at flies
and you're the eyes of this, this

only moment, wobbling up (it could pop
at a touch) as round as O.

> *Oh he strapped up his suitcase of seldom.*
> *He carried it further than most.*
> *His ticket said Forward to Sometime.*
> *He made a small name on the coast.*

Or Was It Baden-Baden?

Days of *millefeuille*, days of *apfelstrudel*,
the sugar-frost rim of a tall glass, lemon-
      ghosted tea...
We meet among mirrors, an infinite regress.
Excuse me, but might it perhaps, where
      could it be
we've met before? At the rail of a cruise ship
threading into the broken rusted ring
      of Santorini

with its stacked card houses, its clinkery steeps,
the iris of its blown-out crater? Or the pink
      Art Deco hotel
on the capsized slab of Poirot Island, the tide
closing in on the sandspit, a perspective
      leading its small self
away, and the sea tractor coming, plash-
paddling with stilt-wheels and its Brasso,
      salt and diesel smell?

Or under the crystal dripping condensations
of which requisitioned spa, the glass dome
      blanched and cool
and folded as the linen of those dove-tail
napkins that always seem about to flirt
      and fly – you, you
in antiseptic mountain light, the inkwell lake
on one hand, on the other, like a shadow cast
      in negative, the too-

clean page of the glacier? And which of us
was it saying: how a face so *ingenue*
      from a mile below
could have its secrets, a climber be lost
alive up there for days – a squall, a crust
      of sugary snow,
he's wombed-in, not even cold; outside,
a new-swept slope, a sense of starting over,
      and who'd be to know?

Stills

She cares for nothing but that caged
capuchin monkey, such a delicate
spoiled beauty that grabs slivers of fruit
peeled for it through the bars
then is fastidious.

*

He has let himself be delivered in a staff car,
with insignia. He feels only contempt
for those who commit such a breach
of etiquette in ignorance. Not him,
he has judged it time for such a move.

*

Oh, she is pale as a papery
Chinese screen. You're not the first to feel
you've seen through almost to the source diffused
that lights it from the other side. My advice?
Sling your hook, kid. Beat it.

*

His mother kept a hornbill with its beak
surgically removed, and fed it mashed nuts.
She kept a cock with no crow. Some say
her taste for such curiosities went further.
Those who know refuse to testify.

*

An imaginary monocle, thick
as the base of a whiskey glass,
screws the old magistrate's face in a wince
like a bad nut or the *agenbite*
of inwit. He was always half a frown.

*

She stares at the splash the young man made
in the deep end and has lost him
then is amazed by the broken shape of him,
greenish and shuddering, foraging sleekly,
half way down the pool.

*

They say he is writing a treatise, the man
at the corner table. There might be a different café round him
that none of us sees. His words fall into place like locusts
settling their wings. The armies that will march
are polishing their boots but do not yet know why.

*

The bell clanged of its own will.
Farm dogs, mongrels, lapdogs from the basket
gathered in packs. Now, the church dome
hangs ruptured by earthquake, now
the sky's own fresco showing through.

*

The girl, one of the implacably
smiling waiters' children, daps a ball
in the bin yard, hour after hour, kicking a bare leg
up and over, muttering a counting game.
If we could catch the language, then we'd know.

*

There will be a dance
tonight, they whisper,
lit by snow light
only, that
and a border-guard's moon.

Written Off

Thud. Like something butting at its pen.
And thud, and again
till it started to splinter, right into my sleep.
No dream,

it was out there
with the hum of heavy motors
and the kind of voices just not right for –
what, as I opened my eyes –

three a.m.? No hint
of what I'd see
looking out... which was nothing
and the street as normal: no one,

only, down by the bridge,
flickered up on the brick,
a blue-then-pink
soft altercation of police light

and the all-night traffic stopped
which was maybe what woke me –
not the noises but the hush between,
like the fault on the negative

greyish-orange between roofs
and the roof of the sky:
a slowly spreading blind spot,
a black Milky Way. No flames,

just the sound-effects. Next morning,
a space in the news, nothing mentioned.
I drove past a buckled nest
of girders on the trading estate –

cleared by lunchtime, the loss written off.
On the next door warehouse wall
were soot shapes like the leaping beasts
of Lascaux, caught in long exposure,

and precisely pyrographed, the one
clear mark, the coil of a refrigeration unit
like a hieroglyph, and two men in suits,
with clipboards – scholars, reading it.

Taking the Waters

Under the steam room,
   burbulous, the bandaged pipes
   are lagged in sacking strips.
Through an unannealed crack
between stone crust and brick
   see inner chambers, darker cisterns,
   cobweb-white deposits crystal-
ising out. Your torch pries in
to thin steam's shifty rising
   close as headlights into fog.
   Fits of the vapours. Clogged
drains, sulphurous. A nether gloom.

§

A municipal drinking fountain, shrunk
   to the size of a wedding cake. Four
   silver faucets with tinkles the colour
of tea, and lukewarm. Raise a thimbleful,
rank as a urine sample; there's a yellow
   dust look on the glass, like moth wings
   give the killing jar. Savour the wince
on both our faces as we lift our nips
like a fine year. Don't think about crisp
   little stink bombs, gone-off lark's
   eggs underfoot. *Your health!* thrown past
our lips, more down-the-hatched than drunk.

§

Shuffled, cut. The small guillotine
  snick of cards stacked. Then the hush
  of the deal, deft, the clickety shunt
of a fresh hand, firmed then fanned
(not sorted, open to the casual glance).
  The bridge school, inner emigrés,
  shrink closer round their green baize
folding tables, in code, plotting
with, about, against each other
  more fondly, more fiercely as the years
  draw in, for the grand slam, the forgotten
cause, the restoration of what old régime.

§

And under all, the curses. Curses,
  pig-lead tokens still tainting the water
  each scratched with its *cri de cœur*.
Marcellus rooked me, damn him. Whoever
had it off with my Fulvia, may he never
  rise to the occasion again. Under the flicker
  of attention spans, the beggars, penny-whistlers,
pavement artists, human statues, under the traffic
of the languages of empire, the automatic
  commentary loop on the open-topped bus
  that talks to itself in the rain... Pity us.
My wife. My gout. My little book of verses.

Some Fine Folly

A true toy castle
on an empty island in an Alp-reflecting lake

without a landing stage...
You'd have to swim it in the privacy of night

dumbstruck with cold
and hope for a moon to show you where to haul ashore.

Beyond the point, that's where
they drowned: the architect, the mason, all their men:

convenient. And the white-haired
mad child-king? Afraid of water. But he brought his court

to gaze all one dull summer
and tell him stories of the life he'd never have out there.

How the seven doors
have no locks and the windows open by ingenious devices

to accept the breath of glaciers
graciously, yet when a storm rises dragging its shadow

like roots, when it rears,
when it roughs up the lake... they shut like eyelids,

for a night, a season, on whatever
they might dream. Imagine: what long-cellared draughts

of longings, pickle-barrels
of what piquant fears. Peering through his spyglass every day

he saw out there nothing but once,
he thought, a small white stump-tailed dog run from the folly

to the water's edge, first yapping
then stockstill, quivering, as if called but made to Stay.

Hydrotherapy.

One day the fashion turned to face it,
the grey animal, shaking its disobliging pelt of spray.
We braced ourselves and walked towards it

keeping our clothes on at first
or with a little house on wheels, a genteel caravan
knee-deep in the Channel, no, a carriage

bogged down in a ford. Something,
at this point in the story, brought us out of the city
to face the wind from the sea –

as if we'd uncovered a wound
that would fester till the salt beast licked it clean,
as if the horizon was a wild spa,

tipping medicinal waters at us
with a taste that made us spit, making our eyes
go red and open grazes smart.

Then it lifted us under the armpits
as we dared wade in. It seemed to like dandling us;
soon we were children again

and could shout, scream and squeal
above its noise, and come out tingling. Even the sand-
melt and undertows called us –

here's me and my dad vaulting
breakers, bull-dancers of Knossos, each leap
deeper, then deeper... Panic:

the bottom was gone. Float,
he called, just in time; the waves bore us in, lordly,
effortless and laughing, and alive.

I couldn't take it personally,
not from a stuff that's so much like part of ourselves,
the same specific gravity as blood.

For all the dead the sea cast up
from the battle of Jutland, there was the wounded sailor
they transfused with pure sea
                              and he lived.

Nick

I can't blame the barber, what with it
being dingy four p.m., what with his life

being difficult, as he told me, as he'd told
the back-and-sides before, what with

the giving up. Disgusting! he cried. Muck!
and kicked the green glass ashtray

at the door, not quite into the street,
like a dog's dish. Huh! If anybody wants,

they can get down on hands and knees.
That's what muck. Leaving his shears tucked

just behind my ear he snatched it back up
rubbing his nose in it, almost. See?

I hate it. *Hate* it. Then, his razor clutched
in trembling hands, turned back to me.

Pantomime Nights

Up past my bedtime

those pantomime nights,
being small in deep streets,
names in vertical lights

climbing hand over hand
to the sky... Then inside:
a foyer as plush as the Grand

with its red padded glow;
clunk of red padded seats; then
the hush at the slow

ebb of houselights; curtains
flouncing up and shuffling
aside their heavy skirts

and there was a near
bright world like a party table
set with everything too clear

to be true, like the mauve-
pansy eyes of the Princess. The sheer-
tighted Principal Boy. Oh,

what was wrong with me? I couldn't wish
them happy ever after: one
of them was *mine*. But which?

*

A real hero, now, would lie in wait
after the show, between stage door
and cheap digs, all ready to hate –

here they come – the stage-door-johnny
wearing *her* like his swagger-stick cane,
his brandy laugh, cravat and easy money.

And to spy, through imaginary keyholes,
him pausing, the connoisseur, at each layer
as he peels her: skirt, jerkin and hose

still on beneath, to silk, to skin,
her inmost smooth and secret folds.
No! It was up to me, to swing in

from the gods one night, in time
to carry her off in mid duet, to roars
and feeble screams behind us,

of the Princess and the crowd.
But I'd reckoned without the Ugly
Sisters – two huge looming jowled

plain-clothes policemen
ripping off bustles and breasts,
two stout defenders of the peace and

the conventions, booming *Time For Bed!*

Mr Biscuit.

It's not that he can't
afford the best,
crisp-edged in crisp dark boxes,

but he buys them
specially: misshapes,
broken moons of gingers, dust-

speckled Jaffa cakes,
stumps of chocolate
fingers, unstuck custard creams,

the last of a line
of ruined Bourbons,
jammy dodgers past their prime. Take,

eat, he spreads them
on a little silver dish
when he invites you back to tea,

a biscuit priest,
while you stare at them,
a puzzle with some pieces missing,

a map of the world
with the continents drifting
apart. In the clock-ticking hush

somehow (but how?) you have to choose.

Prelude, with Feedback
(for Martin)

A decade later, we could have been bad enough for Punk,
jangling the oil cans in Pete's grandad's garage,

taunting our amps into cat-fits of feedback, going at
our guitars with nails, fists, violin bows, bottles, anything

but a crotchet or quaver. Call us a *pop group*, we'd have sued;
we were a band, going on for a troupe, no, a caravan,

all the girls we fancied tagging on as 'dancers', their boyfriends,
all older than us, given a bongo each and told to beat it;

they stayed. We had percussion like the drummers of Burundi.
Too far west to be West Coast, in a greyish dockyard town,

we were the Underground, knitted at home out of airwaves
unravelled from off-shore lightships, albums smuggled in

with names like Moby Grape and Iron Butterfly. And us? *Wasteland,*
yes, like T.S. Eliot; even our English teachers had to half approve.

We had media; these were the days of light shows, gloopy
oil slides like those egg-yolk table lamps, period stuff. Yes,

we were period, high-minded, innocent, psychedelic
as in Aldous Huxley, shelling out at festivals for sugar cubes

that packed a massive hit of... well, sugar. Smoking anything,
nutmeg, dried banana leaves, on the offchance. Tapping a leak

from the chemists' warehouse where all the dropout drummers
happened to work – Mandrax, it made your legs go out from under,

thump. Was that it? you thought, lying there. It seemed it was.
Just grown up, now we could be kids again – in Pounds Park

on the swings after dark, fumbling joints. Nothing could harm us,
tripping on the cliffs at Looe, pursued by luminous thistles;

we were weightless, so how could we fall? Now and again
someone else we heard of died, or lost their mind.

And you were out there, Martin, at the heart of it,
slightly apart, the all-night operator in the listening post

on the wires to America, up with Ginsberg, the Black Panthers,
Warhol, souls on ice, who killed Kennedy, burn baby burn,

you were out there alone; maybe we all were, but you, you
were visible, out by the mike, light glinting on your unhip glasses.

None of us got the girls we wanted. Our amps and gear got nicked
on the eve of our big break – most of it was borrowed – leaving
        some of us

to join the folk revival; you, the revolution. Am I making this up?
We were making ourselves up, talking hour after hour

after gigs in Pete's mini, by the dashboard lights. We'd nearly
grasped it, something, if we could only find the words –

scratching those songs out, bits of Trotsky, bits of blues,
and yes, the night Barbara, our convent school girl singer

I never did kiss, yelled at the cidery crowd: *Shut up and listen,
this is a poem, the best fucking poem I've read.* And beyond

words, just once in a while in a night in a daze of forgetting
our scarcely a music lesson's notes to scrape together,

we'd play, climbing on each other's shoulders, stepping
off as an updraught caught us and we didn't fall, we flew.

The Road to Nada

It's coming back. How he stepped out at you, without moving,
out of the scratches and scrawls on the loading bay wall,
one moment a shadow, then he had one of his own.

That was two hundred miles back, on the far side of hours
on end pouring down the highway, town lights trailing off behind
till there's nothing but windvanes and wires on their poles,

a flash of thorn scrub or its shadows streaking off backwards
like things taking fright. Then the mountains, leaning into bends
and there against a boulder, wasn't that a glimpse of him, side on,

always, now you come to think, facing one way, north, was it, or left,
in his blanket like one of the Previous People, as stiff as a hieroglyph,
always in profile, looking off, not at us, not the future, which is what

maybe did for them? Still, but lifting something cradled to his lips,
a clay pipe, no, a shrill reed whistle – not that you'd hear
through the glass and the gears and the radio's road movie soundtrack

but you knew how it must be: like ripped air, like wheelspin in grit,
a bird shriek. So next time you'd see the shape your lights throw off him
on the back wall of a gutted petrol station, its price sign still swinging,

you'd see it like wings. Then the last twist in the mountains, a hairpin
that lays it out wide as a sigh: in their twenty-mile grid on the plain,
the lights of home, out, down, beyond the warning arrow signs,

the busted railings where some coach or truck went through,
the blank shale wall. Wing-shadows spread now, as you swerve
he turns. His flared beak. Blank hawk's eye. It's coming back to you.

Ghost Ranch: Georgia O'Keefe

How far can you get
from the attics, ateliers, insect buzz
and shove of openings, private views?

Here, there's nothing but studio,
inside, outside. Nothing.
                    But this face

with its hardening angles,
bank-clerk's hair, has grown mannish
as a frontier woman's. How far

can you get from iris throats,
swallow-you-in-one-gulp mauves,
from night blacks, pollen sulphurs

that enfold you like a child
in mother's wardrobe? And why
should it come as a surprise

if bare rock opens for her
like a flower, giving up colours
like scents to the sun – not like boom-

and-bust-in-one-day desert flora
but slowly, hard come by, the bloom
of the whole West? Oh, spare me

the poetry, her eyes say. Look
till you are what you look at:
landscape.
            Gulches.
                    Going blind

as if from too much sun glare
those eyes narrow on some distance
I can't grasp. I haven't got that far.

Life in the Glass Age

I

There must have been a sun
and somewhere a horizon
and they met. That much we guess,

the way the light moves
from the red to the blue
end of the spectrum, through the glass-

floored mezzanines, indoor
potted palms and furniture
in mid air; now, at dusk, the sleepless

glitter-globes in strings
are bubbles rising,
glinting on marble that's tooled to a gloss

like a fast shallow river,
no ripples, sheeting over
darker pebbles you could almost touch.

In the concourse, like valves
of a heart, stand two halves
of a night sky we can step right into; each

face of cloudy split agate
knows the other like a secret.
We approach together then, as at a lych-

gate, step through one
by one. Why this is done
is not for us to say. We know that much.

II

Glimpsed, it's gone
as you look: an earth-tone
that, if you could follow it, teasing

reflection apart
from refraction through
the depthless planes of glazing,

might be raw
or burnt siena, bloodshot
filaments of madder – not just light

singing arias
to itself but something
anyone might stumble on, say a late

shift worker
opening an unmarked
door, into a sudden damp of stone,

a reticence
of mudbrick alleys shading
back and in. Look... Too late. Gone.

III

A cargo cult? A weightless grid
of economics, as one theory holds,
dropped on a bare hill from a clear sky?
The shapes of desire? Or suppose

all this was here before us,
in the way the light behaved
that made some nomads halt
with a sense that they'd arrived

at a place already built but not
yet visible – to be pieced together
in time, from sun and wall and shadow
like the nicked edge of a razor,

from a slowly gathering buff glow
in courtyards seen through passageways
which on the unpremeditated
cusp of evening folds the place

inside out in one deft movement
like a child's game, *here's-the-church-
and-here's-the-steeple*, folding
all of us inside it so each arch

    frames sky, not dark but Prussian blue
    too intense to look at. As residents
    we're used to this, accepting what's
    before our eyes, the *prima facie* evidence.

    IV

Good morning. And how was your stay?
The light will be with you shortly,
and a choice of colours.

Rosy-fingered Dawn with her overalls on
is sprucing down the mall,
fluffing dust from the light wells.

Cleaners glide out slow as swans
over pools of polished marble
on the hum of their sweeping machines.

The whole house of cards rebuilds itself.
Glass lift doors flex and sigh,
and all the many-angled selves

we caught reflected in windows
with the night outside
are thinning like the stage ghost trick.

You saw them? This much we can say:
it'll all come out in the blue
then pink wash of *Have a nice day*.

Strange But True

Yes, there were witnesses – not just the morning-after
no-good slumped against the jetty,
but an up-for-the-action stevedore or two

and the captain of the steam crane, just tamping
his first pipe of Old Mouldy, and the waitress
in the truckers' hang-out shrivelling the first eggs of the day

when she lost her gaze off into six o'clock distance,
then cried out. When help came there was nothing to see.

This much was agreed: it was all far off, but not
too far to swear to, where the estuary begins to lose
track of its shores and has its moods of tide and flow:

heavy water, the weight of the raw umber silt in it
banking up foam rucks, dangerously still.
Even the dredging barge goes warily. But there they were:

the rafts, a slow convoy of them, raftsmen leaning
to their makeshift rudders, and such heaps of what

lashed to the heaving decks, it was like a clearance,
like when the old Senora with the mad chihuahuas died
without heirs. A city, though, this was a city,

its moveables, wardrobes, tallboys, mangles, a fine iron gate
and an altar screen, fountains, lamp posts, toilet bowls...
What trunks of small fondnesses we can only guess at.

But there was no city up there, in the interior.
This has been proved. At most there might float down

a waterlogged tree trunk, black flank wallowing
over like a whale. Besides, where could they be moving on to
with that set look, that calm, and not sparing

a glance for the town? Maybe they didn't hear us,
all waving and hailing as if something depended
on making them turn, at least to shout a name.

But there were witnesses. I know, with my own eyes,
and my friend Chris was there; he read it with me

in the Wilco's Wonders column of our *Strange But True.*
Nowadays there'll be web sites. I don't need to look;
I know there'll be the same tale, maybe last year,

the name of the town changed, and the witnesses...
If they'd looked with good enough binoculars, there
on the last raft, gazing at the quays, at the hullaballoo

of waving people, as if all he saw was virgin forest,
they'd have seen a small boy with a pile of dog-eared magazines.

Mappa Mundi

I

In the land of mutual rivers,
it is all a conversation: one flows uphill, one flows down.
Each ends in a bottomless lake which feeds the other
and the boatmen who sail up, down, round and round
never age, growing half a day older, half a day younger
every time... as long as they never step on land.

II

In the land of always autumn
people build their houses out of fallen leaves
and smoke, stitched together with spiders' webs.
At night they glow like parchment lanterns and the voices
inside cluster to a sigh. Tell us a story, any story, except
hush, please, not the one about the wind.

III

In the land where nothing happens twice
there are always new people to meet;
you just look in the mirror. Echoes learn to improvise.
So it's said... We've sent some of the old
to investigate, but we haven't heard yet. When we
catch up with them, we might not know.

IV

In the land of sounds you can see
we watch the radio, read each other's lips, dread
those audible nightfalls. We pick through the gloom
with one-word candles *home... however... only... soon...*
while pairs of lovers hold each other, speechless,
under the O of a full black moon.

V

In the land of hot moonlight
the bathing beaches come alive at midnight.
You can tell the famous and rich by their silvery tans
which glow ever so slightly in the dark
so at all the best parties there's a moment when the lights go out
and you, only you, seem to vanish completely.

VI

In the land of migratory words
we glance up, come the season, at telegraph wires
of syllables in edgy silhouette against a moving sky
like code, unscrambling. Any day now they'll fall into place
and be uttered. Then the mute months. The streets
without names. The telephone that only burrs.

We Are the Twittering Machine

(after Paul Klee)

It may be the city settling
round us, turning three times widdershins
    like a dog in the long
grass of instinct, that cranks the machine.
    Cam-shafted on an axle
oiled by the last round, we bob up and utter
    each our call-sign, some
just an audible comma, o*h?, uh-huh*. Like frequencies
    lost into radio space
taking chat shows to Alpha Centauri, we scribble
    our marks on the air;
they stay scratched on the pink fug of sunset
    that's shading away
and away till I can hardly see the terrace
    let alone the view
we came for – blame it on pollution,
    blame it on Paul Klee –
till we're putting the world to rights
    by a shack with no roof
in a dustbowl where a windvane clacks and squeaks
    with the voice of a bird,
no, of five or six birds of our different species.
    Try as we may to tune
our breaths together, it comes out as *he, she, you,*
    me, all our asymmetric creaks.

Losing It

What was it, that if *one* can,
in the old Guinness ad, think what toucan
    do? And what is it that, gone,
a word leaves? Something like a token
    of obscure esteem, or love, or
sense, like the dusting of stale talc in
    an empty dresser drawer –
ungraspable, and yours for the taking

    into that forgetfulness we all
might come to. Then we'll see what two can
    truly do. I think the word
was *satisfy*, but I could be mistaken.
    Shut me up, love. Hold me.
Sometimes I can't hear myself for talking.

Ithaca

There's one road in,
a there and back again affair –
each new arrival flagged an hour off

by a scarf of dust
blown from the hairpin
in the limestone up against the sky

or a bicker of birds
going up, discommoded
from small carrion. It's the job they're in

keeping the hillside white
as a sailor's daymark coming
over his blue horizon: what he's held out for,

landfall, one happy return.
Ithaca Shores: Retirement Villas…
where the self-unpicking tapestries of lives

      become and un-
          become at leisure. Time
            to turn back

           to a kind of adolescence, that fidgety edge again,
               staring into a mirror with our own
                  once-older faces in it

          watching gravely, knowing what we'd have
            no choice but be, and what we're slipping
              into, back over the edge:

        a hindsight childhood not carefree but cool-
           eyed as you come to notice
             children often are, as if

      they've seen more than is called for already –
          fair enough, they've stored it
            like suitcases packed

        for somebody else's idea of a holiday.
           Just load the boot and take
             that one road in,

            a there and back affair.

Wickanninnish

We could have felt cheated, after everything:
the all-night gnat-hum of the neon on the ferry-port motel;
next day, the nose-to-grindstone climbs in low gear,

hairpins, the occasional achievement of a roadhouse
(pricey, grudging). Our van sat steaming amongst sleek RVs
with names like Overlord, glinting suburbs on wheels,

kitted out as if for lunar landings. And somewhere
it happened – no, *had* happened. Which was it, the particular
rise among the general woods and bluffs and screes?

I'd imagined a viewpoint – say, a café called The Wild
Surmise. We sensed it in the gearbox – look, we were going
over fifty. The light in the woods, in the mist, wasn't less

but different – more *inward* – brighter mosses glowing
through the grey. In-, on- and downward, the lie of the land.
The idea of a valley had been deepening unseen

though the stream left the roadside just minutes ago.
Signs: how the lichen strands hung on the firs, more, tweedier,
on *that* side as if scenting a breeze we couldn't feel yet,

seaward. Sea? No, the *ocean*. No ferry-ports there –
even the whale watching trip we were told we must take
barely scratched it – four hours straight out, four

straight back in the hopes of a glimpse of a whale
as if that might be big enough to speak for vastness. We'd left
something behind – something, and also the sense of why

that thing had mattered. The mountains we'd toiled for
felt small – no harm in that: they were *our* mountains now, but
small, like some other time's news. Instead... this other.

Ocean. An entire half world of water. That wasn't ours.
Not even to view. All the way down it was trees, cloud, rock
bluffs, shifting. A swathe of strip-logged hillside

was grief that would heal. Then sundown, town lights,
street names like someone else's memories: down Seaplane
Base Road was a bend of dark river; astride it, the cannery

bright and clanking. In a haze of morning the Pacific Rim
National Park was still only a name plate we'd parked under,
still an act of faith... till I stepped out. It was everywhere,

close, a steady scouring in the air, like waves and wind
attempting the word for the place, the old one: *Wickanninnish.*
Now I see myself running through sparse twiggy pines,

toward the smooth rise of the dunes, sand slipping, time
melting under my feet as I run, and they're calling,
my family, friends, behind me, and I'm glad but

don't look back, and I guess that the last thing we'd know
might be that: not quite the ocean, but the moment
just before...

(for HD, going over fifty...)

First Night

And then the night was flush with fireworks, like some kind of eve,
a parasol of cyclamen-pink flares, and everyone gazing up, straight up,
    little asterisks bright in their eyes

and what was the occasion, no one seemed to know –
with the air of an opening, champagne laid on by an unknown sponsor
    and though everyone had memories

right up to the moment when they'd stepped into the smoke-edged air,
it was as if they'd never met each other's. Anything anybody said
    was new. The wonder was, the stories

seemed to tally. Am I the only one, thought Gina, wondering what,
what if they didn't? One slip was all it would take… So when
    she overheard Mal saying much the same

to friends who laughed just like they laughed at everything –
another bang, the way it set off dogs, babies and car alarms –
    she knew this was meant, her and him,

and as glitter-green shivered the bare trees, ooh said everybody
and she told him, breathless, and he grabbed her by both hands;
    they both began to laugh,

a different laughter from the mates around them, fierce and fearful
as if they'd strayed to the top of the tallest building and strolled
    hand in hand to the unfenced edge

with eyes fixed on each other. You mean, he said, I could say
anything? Try, she said, and squatting in a doorway he began
    on the day he'd been found, a phone-

box foundling in a pizza carton – no, a changeling – no,
a lone twin, searching for his other, till, yes, now… Flash,
    went the sky. Before the bang,

before the long fizzles of bronze, they saw each other's faces
from another angle, in another dispensation, where who knows
    what other thing was true, and how

they'd met, quite, they'd forgotten but yes, they could do it
    again, yes, again and again…

The Key to the Kingdom

It's not exile, homes and families behind
us, where we meet. It happens anywhere,
        now: a stateless
state of no name, quietly seceding
from the crumbling empires round us,

without stamps or Eurovision entries.
No one does it with a rough guide in a week.
        You inhabit it
or nothing. Like this: in a pavement cafe
you blink and you seem to surprise them,

the crowd, all its separate faces at once,
coming out of solution like crystals,
        like a rush of starlings
or the breeze that lifts the canvas awning
now and dents your cappuccino froth

with a crisp little sound. And that's it:
between breaths, just between you and me
        as if, yes,
QED. You are received. This is
the freedom of the city, and the key

to the kingdom, and its borders ripple
outwards like a frill of breaking wave
        onto flat sand,
a wavering line already fading leaving
spume-flecks high and dry,

a prickling on your palm; you're five
years old, looking up at the whole sea,
        unsure:
                will you laugh or cry?

Tales of the Forest

They say the real Bluebeard's Castle
is just up the road from here
    but then so do twenty other villages
    between the airport and the border zone.

A coach leaves on the hour.
We could go, we two, among the dozens.
    There's a buffet thrown in, braised
    hearts and strawberries and the local brew.

It would mean getting out of our bed
in the Honeymoon Suite: a curt
    start after breakfast and the guide
    with matching lipstick, clipboard, scarlet blazer

wants us organised in ethnic groups;
she can swivel from language to language,
    click, click. All that puts me off
    is that one must be English,

not the patter (like rain moving in
in the night as we wake to taste each other
    one more time) of a language
    we don't have to understand. No,

let's drift to the dining room,
asking for breakfast at midday,
    stay late in the bar, past
    some notion of bedtime, just to tease,

touching toes beneath the table
as we let Mister Been-here-before
    buttonhole us with his tale –
    of a friend of a friend, in a hire car,

driving through the forest when a boar,
a real wild one, ran straight out; he swerved
    but caught the beast a cruncher –
    like an upholstered boulder, he said –

and he span off in the ditch,
his radiator hissing, the whole wing
   crumpled in; the boar staggered,
    then ran on, and three piglets came after,

straight over, back into the underbrush,
leaving just the hiss of steam
   and his heart, and a dim sense
    none of this had ever been.

The Word

Drowsing afterwards,
grown man in a baby-nap,
he's conscious, just,

of made-together moistures
dried on skin, the his-and-hers-
ness of it... not to mention

the slapdash of clouds, the almost-
stillness unpulled curtains frame
as he fades...

    ...and blinks awake
to the same light at a different
slant across the bedspread,

and above him (he can't take
it in, too near) and intent
with no expression he can name,

her face. *Sssh:* a fingertip
dabbed to her tongue.
Deft as a vicar at the font,

with a lick at a time, fast as spit dries,
she's writing the word, on the dip
of his breastbone,

      spelling what
his skin can't read, not
quick enough, and she won't say.

Come the Day

After months of little wonders, jeopardies
like plush desserts in bistros, festivals
            we found ourselves inventing daily,
plucking them like new exotic weeds
that may come to be normal, given global warming
(think of the passion-flower seedling withered
      in the tindery thatch of Russian vine;
      months later there's a mauve and cream
pale apparatus, a radar dish, no, five or six
of them, up in the vine and roses, launched
      like fireworks)…
                        After all, comes the day
dragging home down a back street with bags
and I'm stopping to look but not much
      at the stiff slouch of cranes, the gruffed-
      up patch of nothing yet like houses
where the way-back left-wing bookshop finally
came down. (The walls hardly needed a push,
      just permission; to grub up the cellars took weeks.)
      A weariness is waiting like a local dog, a stray
that knows me and comes dumbling over,
head hung, half blind, can't be shooed,
      it has my scent.
                        Back home, how to explain
      these carrier bags stretched out of shape
I upend at your feet, and nothing in them?
Only the damp dog smell, the shadowing
      of afternoons, the place where the soul goes
      slumming it, clean out of bright new pennies,
slumping now on the rug as if something
scuffed, something drab and that won't
      wipe its feet was needful, also needful,
      in the furnishing of what will last, a home.

Iceland

Every coupled-up love-match is a foreign-speaking country, but theirs
had something awesome in it. Something scary. Like the day
he rang mid-morning at the office; *Right*, she said and, not precipitate,
worked till lunchtime, then left a note stuck on her screen:
Gone To Iceland. We tried to make a joke of it right through the afternoon
but knew – oh, we'd seen them together – this wasn't about frozen food.
By teatime we'd remembered what she'd said once, glancing
at a supplement, about his fishing, and mountains. There they were
in a hut at the end of a fjord, if they have fjords, by a glacier stream
and him sitting, in the kind of time only they could give each other,
under saga-wide skies, skies with the breath of Hekla in them, her
bringing the Thermos out steaming like a geyser, him with a hook
forged for a hero, dredging the glacier's tail, the blue ice-clefts,
for all the time it took, as the fish came downhill at glacier speed,
ten years, a hundred, unerringly into the path of his gaffe
and then he'd hoist it back in triumph to her, for the freezer
     just as if they'd been to Iceland after all.

Retreat

Stepped aside from our separate lives
together, in the garden, we are not alone –
St Francis skulking in the laurels, and a hack,
pause, pant, hack: Father Cormac coming through

with a billhook, in shirtsleeves. It's all he can do,
he says, to keep the paths open, not to mention
the rabbits that crater the thin grass
like a small bombardment night by night.

If he had his way, he'd pave it all,
the lawn around the grotto. Lourdes
in local fluted limestone, it has Bernadette
on her knees while, a statue adored

by a statue, Mary lifts her pale blue
slightly crumbling plaster eyes.
A smudge of mould muddies her hem
as if she'd got down to it, taking her turn

trampling wild garlic and bluebell stalks
crisp as asparagus, or raking out the pond
whose plaster heron tilts askew
over embers of goldfish, where the surface

shows as one reflection me and you,
statues, arms to shoulders, arms to waist,
in attitudes of blessed and blessing, that
old miracle. And maybe they'll be kind,

the saints we can't quite credit – not
to make us see, too much, our wildered paths,
our muddied hems, the crumbling plaster
we touch round each other's lips and eyes.

Pound

Under the railway arch there's a small
black flood, chopping away from wheels
and brake lights. You slop through
to night and streetlight-yellowed walls,

an iron gate propped open, padlock-
chain still on it. There's a lit hut
in the dark yard – *Please Report
To Reception* – and a phone-box

space to squint through glass and grille.
Most people want to smash the face
that looks out, you can tell. The undertaker's
manner that he wears, in jail-

house slang, it's *dogface*, studiously
lax, nothing to snag the least reaction.
The lowered voice between the bars
conducts you through fixed penalties,

rights of appeal. Sign here. It's the start
of a bad shift, through till midnight,
with drink on his breath. Through lit
blinds and wire mesh, his silhouette

gets up slow to operate the inner gate
with its wire-curler trim. Remote
control: a bolt clunks, wires tense.
CCTV clocks you while you wait.

Inside, not much: a car park with a shame-
faced look. Three guys in hoods
stand round their car, kicking its hubcaps,
squinnying in, as if it's not the same,

smells wrong, like a baby bird replaced
in the old nest, human-tainted, or a soul
misdelivered to hereafter, weighed
out wrong. It's just a job to Dog-Face.

The Edge of Summer

Down and out of the forest
something left its traces on the morning,
        some days, then not for a week.
        We'd have time to forget,
almost, the shredded stems,
the garbage strewn and looted.
        Then the heart-slump at first light:
        look, a trail going heavily, big-pawed
back up into out-of-sight.
Or, stranger, fading out mid-way...

                    *

Our life was a house by the lake
and all we'd rented for the season:
        the First People's petroglyphs pecked
        in a wave-slopped cliff as if they'd known
someone would have to float a shaky
pontoon boardwalk for the likes of us;
        the big-bellied flying boat ending its days
        with plump pedaloes nuzzling under its wings;
our hours together in a kind of praise
of... what, it seemed like tempting fate to say.

                    *

Us, on the verandah: hammock afternoons
or that time that's always a late breakfast,
        time like coffee resinously brewed,
        time we made for each other, vying
so we might both arrive together,
cafetières in hand, to wait on two
        figments of a leisure so complete
        they had become transparent, us-
shaped gestures, us-shaped weight
in the hammocks. Us, the servants, waiting.

                    *

One night I caught you sleepless, and knew
without asking. Was it out there now?
      you were wondering. Its breath in the yard.
      Its sad smell in the morning. How much closer
might it come? I was wondering too:
how long before you said *Enough*.
      Let's move on. We caught each other
      wondering. That's when the holiday sat down
between us, like a grown-up daughter
first seeing her parents ageing, a little afraid.

         *

No more said. But from that night
the locals would greet us (How could they know?
      Could *it* have told them?) like residents. Now,
      these Autumn mornings, we gaze at the lake,
bright mist rising, and hardly need say
what we see as it shreds and clears: no
      holiday, but gleaming shed roofs, the haze
      of the motorway spur, home, the place we began
and yet over it all is what could be the play
of water and light. Which seems set to remain.

Nocturne

Of all the times in all the nights in all the world
to have a blackbird singing... Of all the monochrome

stills of small hours smuggled as the clocks go forward
stealing a march on us, into the notion of spring...

Of all the side-slips into half waking, into half now
like a module, one bed's width, with its own supplies of air

and wonder – or like a lifeboat adrift for weeks
where we've rigged up a tenting of polythene sheet

creased so our breaths condense and trickle back down
to a taste flat as battery water, just a hint of tar,

salt and Swarfega... Of all these night-moves,
these casual pick-ups of logic, quite fuzzy and plausible,

that lead down a back street of connections
where the one lamp fizzes orange, melting wall,

roof, binbag, me, you and a low cat into its dream
and one blackbird can't sleep, and we should really

do something about the thin curtains that let in a glimmer
to touch in your cheek, eyes closed, eyelids quivering,

lips in the consideration of a smile... Of all the faces,
I had to wake into yours, at last, here's looking at you,

looking all the ages that you've ever been
and that blackbird, time switch blown by the always

not quite dawn, in the scrub of the railway cutting
sings as if there's no tomorrow, or no night between.

The Kingdom of Corrugated

On the fringes always, it was, in the corner of your eye
and withdrawn when you looked, like an offer or a hint you'd
        never take,

not yet. There was the green-peeling scout hut, like a last stand
of the 1950s, in a square stockade of ropey spruces with a
        padlocked gate

and miles of bare moor all around. There was the biscuity rust
of the Anderson shelter your spade took a bite of, in the vague
        rockeried mound

at the bottom of the garden, among plate sherds, glass and
        builders' rubble.
There was the feeling that you didn't want to look inside. And
        now again

where you gaze out every morning, glancing from the bathroom
        mirror
to the sky, as if comparing something, there are the roofs, up the
        back lane,

of the lock-up garages, sheet overlapping sheet, and bird droppings
        and thumb-
thick caterpillars of bright moss that seek into and clog the runnels.
        Squint

and it's a landscape from a mile up: rucked strata and seepings of
        green,
so much sameness and not quite, to flummox the eye. You're
        flying, no, being

flown deep into that country. Where are they taking you? That
        strip down there,
yes, that clitter of flat roofs. The epitome of outback. They're
        letting you in

to the secret. This is the capital (pop. 20), the command post of
        the undeclared
world. It has boulders as big as a shack and too crumbly to build
        with; trees,

poison thorns, that fray like hard string. Get a splinter and you'll
        swell up
bad as snake bite. Make yourself at home. Midday, even the air is
        corrugated,

the horizon goes wobbly with heat stroke, it bangs off the flat roofs.
        Sit
and gradually you'll see how an end wall, no one in particular, is
        gathering blue

grey, zinc dustiness, tincture of pearl. (You could get nostalgic,
        almost, for red.
Here, nothing ever rusts.) You'll see the sense of each square
        compound

fenced in corrugated, though the ground inside is just the same as out.
How that's the glory of it. You'll stay out high cold nights to stare

at the glasspaper sky and feel the planet rubbing down to dust.
        Or when a moon
creaks up, bigger than you could imagine, all the roofs in town
        (pop.20)

are frost, are unthinkable snow, and well, to be the centre of the
        world
would be just plenty, but this is the icing on the cake.

As When

Here's one for the album
like a day that might just be the last
   of the season, when a thinning
   into brightness of the early mist
puts a pennanted steamboat
by the lakeside jetty, but no shore.
   Do we have time for a Homeric simile?
   Let's hope. It is as when

after hours of one horizon,
with the cruise ship paying out its wake
   on a dry-white, let's say Chablis,
   sea, look, there's an island,
close. It's where it must have been
for hours, but wasn't. What to do
   with these travellers' tales?
   Is it enough, just being there

or should we wrangle with the natives?
Don't you suspect them, slightly,
   with their guile of seeming just surprised
   coming out of the forest with
is that a unicorn? slung on a pole
by its delicate hooves, feebly swiping
   at their feet, never wounding,
   but dragging a script in the dust

from which they say a wise man
might read the future. And the shriek
   of the beast offstage, its last bubbling,
   isn't it a bit *too much*
and this wide-eyed gravity of theirs
a bit too knowing? No,
   I can't prove anything. All I'm asking
   is: after we've gone

and no one's looking, do they stay
in silhouette against that skyline?
    Does that sun persist in setting
    and do they down tools and speculate
about us, what brought us out
of nowhere? Are they still astonished,
    gently, by each other, the way we
    can be, waking, on this kind of day?

Old enough to know better, they're both old enough to know
    that it doesn't get nakeder than this,
palm by palm, slipping hand into hand in public places

like a compact, a secret that's safe
    as, aged fifteen, it never seemed. How could they have known
then (who'd have dared tell them?)

going shy and headlong towards something vaguely *more* –
    the lips, or the lips slightly parted,
or, whole levels deeper in, the major arcana of the bra strap

or the first astonishment
    of knicker elastic which, when he'd forged his way in,
was *homely*, like his sister's –

rushing on past this moment, holding on too tight
    or betrayed by the sweat of his palm
or surprised at her slim hand feeling bony, not quite opening,

an unripe feeling, *granted,* that was all,
    not given? Who'd have said *This is it:* the palms not touching,
not quite, on a space between

like a lark's egg, with small stirrings in it as if they,
    together, they could incubate it,
against all the odds, but it's going to take both of them,

their palms cupped round it just so, they mustn't forget?

The White Machines

They come low, out of nowhere,
and silent, the air parting finely
as ham pale from the butcher's slice.
    Night after night.

They are frictionless, bodiless,
all wing, crisp folds, origami,
slick and snugly nested as the blades
    of a Swiss Army knife.

They could go anywhere, at will
but choose these dreams where everyone
runs out to gape. If these are warplanes
    it's technology so rarified

that Friend or Foe has ceased to matter.
They draw us like the plume of smoke
down a cordoned-off street, the warnings
    Keep calm, stay inside

we ignore. We can't move, until one
clips a housetop. It cartwheels
and rips into papery flames.
    This time, before

I wake, I'll pull it from the wreckage,
this whatever, charred or scarred
for life. Yes, I think life is what
    it comes here for.

All the Weather You Can Think Of

No, I said, this wasn't what we ordered

but it was delivered to our window: dawn
came with a flash, then slow considered thunder,

then a cresting wave of wind, hail chittering,
some dark like night again, and all of a sudden

the sun! Six impossible things
before breakfast... where the TV weather girl

was being sweet and bright and keen
like a child with something for the Nature Table

though we all know what she's in
is a blue space, and she's gesturing

in trust that everything needful
to make sense of her is being digitally mastered

in. This wasn't what we ordered. Don't
you know what day it is? I asked her

with the sound down, and her hands and eyes
said Yes, said Yes to everything

as if she would have married me
and all of us, us and our weather, there and then.

Which sent me out into silvery streets,
with flashes of discarded sunlight everywhere:

pavements, gutters, passing windscreens –
here, blue sky, and there a black cloud propped

against a near horizon, and a rainbow stump,
just the base of one under construction,

like more than a miracle (for God it's just
too simple), like the work of human hands

together, our joined hands, today.
This wasn't what we ordered

but we won't say no.